Presented To

_____

By

_____

Date

_____

THE
POCKET DEVOTIONAL
for WOMEN

Honor Books
Colorado Springs, Colorado

The Pocket Devotional for Women
ISBN 1-56292-877-5
Copyright © 2002 by Honor Books
4050 Lee Vance View
Colorado Springs, CO 80918

Compiled by Angie Kiesling

Introduction

You owe it to yourself to take more time to reflect on God's principles, but how do you find the time? With *The Pocket Devotional for Women* you can feast on God's Word accompanied by a pertinent quotation and an upbeat reflection to help you apply these life-transforming principles to your life. Each day you will experience the uplifting inspiration that comes from reflecting on God's truth regularly.

The convenient size of this devotional makes it perfect to put in a purse or bag for those odd moments of the day, standing in line, waiting on a client, or over a cup of coffee on a break. It's small enough to put on the nightstand for that last quiet moment as you let go of the day's worries and let sleep overtake you. No matter where your available moments occur, *The Pocket Devotional for Women* is small enough to carry along, just in case. Take it with you each day, and experience the life transformation that occurs when His truth soaks into your heart.

Be more concerned with
what God thinks about
you than what people
think about you.

Our aim is to please him always
in everything we do, whether we
are here in this body or away from
this body and with him in heaven.

2 CORINTHIANS 5:9 TLB

Living for an Audience of One

As women, we're quick to measure ourselves against society's standards, even when those standards seem impossibly high. No area is left unscrutinized: beauty, career, physical fitness, possessions, relationships—even our spirituality. But the treadmill of perfection-seeking leaves us winded and joyless, and we wonder, *Is there more to life than this?*

When we live our lives for an audience of one— God—something remarkable happens. Suddenly, the things we desperately sought don't matter anymore, and unexpected things that truly delight drop into our laps at just the right time. Our new agenda leaves little time for worrying.

Sometime today, stop to thank God for His presence in your life. The simple act of remembering your Audience will lead you into some delightful adventures and keep you focused on the things that matter most.

Be a God-pleaser, not a people pleaser.

Life is a coin. You can
spend it any way
you wish, but you can
only spend it once.

*What is your life? It is even
a vapor that appears for a little
time and then vanishes away.*

JAMES 4:14 NKJV

One Go-around

Reaching for the brass ring on the merry-go-round was a playful quest, and your odds of grasping the ring were good simply because you went around and around many times. Your painted horse brought you within reach of that ring every time.

With life, however, we get only one go-around, one chance to live our dreams and chase a ring of gold. Knowing this, the mundane tasks we perform mechanically every day take on new meaning. Missed opportunities stand out clearly. Small acts of kindness become sacred rituals.

Seen from the vantage point of eternity, our lives really are a vapor, a drifting fog that soon vanishes from earth. But when we offer our lives to God, that vanishing point is just the doorway into a more wonderful reality—Heaven, where another ring, a crown of gold, awaits us.

Live today as if it were your last.

A diamond is a chunk
of coal that made
good under pressure.

Consider it all joy . . . when you
encounter various trials, knowing
that the testing of your faith
produces endurance. And let
endurance have its perfect result,
so that you may be perfect and
complete, lacking in nothing.

JAMES 1:2-4 NASB

The Value of Pressure

When you stop to admire a diamond in a jeweler's window, do you ever imagine the chunk of coal it once was? We put a high price tag on quality, but often we forget what process it took to achieve that worth. A diamond takes time and pressure to showcase its best features. After all, that expensive, flawless stone started out as a crumbly chunk of carbon.

Life throws us curveballs now and then. God knew these trials would put the squeeze on us much the same way time and pressure shape a chunk of coal. A metamorphosis takes place, and something wonderful emerges.

Remember that you are a work in progress. Like any good artisan, God uses His hammer and chisel to shape a thing of beauty. And He has promised not to leave His work undone.

Troubles may come, but they only increase your value.

What sunshine is to flowers,
smiles are to humanity.
They are but trifles, to be
sure; but, scattered along
life's pathway, the good
they do is inconceivable.

*A happy heart makes
the face cheerful.*

PROVERBS 15:13 NIV

Scattering Smiles

Here's a great way to subtract years from your face: smile a lot! A happy face always looks younger than a frowning one, and at the same time you just may lighten someone's load—even if only for a moment. Everyone responds to a cheery disposition, and a smile is often quite contagious. Why not spread a few "germs" around today?

It's never wise to scrimp on smiles, because down the road we will reap multiplied goodwill with the smiles we give out today. Those small kindnesses scattered a thousand different directions will yield an unexpected bounty of returned goodwill and favors.

Even when "down" days come your way, train your face to turn frowns upside down. The conscious decision to smile is always worth the effort. And it just may chase the blues away for you and for others.

Your face is a billboard showing
what's inside your heart.

Our days are identical suitcases—all the same size—but some people can pack more into them than others.

Be very careful, then, how you live—not as unwise but as wise, making the most of every opportunity.

EPHESIANS 5:15-16 NIV

Making Our Day Count

Budgeting our time sounds like one more item on our endless to-do list, but this piece of advice comes from a Source we can trust: God. How do you live "as wise, making the most of every opportunity"? How do you pack your "suitcase" so that it's full but not popping the hinges every day?

Making moments count begins with realizing that our lives are not our own but gifts from God. When we give ourselves to Him—in the form of blessing others and sowing seeds of faith—even mundane days take on a sacred quality. Busyness is transformed into purposeful accomplishment, a fullness that overflows the heart. We go beyond just coping.

If we start the day asking God to order our steps each moment, He will prove His strength in the midst of our weakness.

Every moment, every breath you take,
can become a gift to be treasured.

When you flee
temptations, don't leave
a forwarding address.

Now flee from youthful lusts and
pursue righteousness, faith, love
and peace, with those who call
on the Lord from a pure heart.

2 TIMOTHY 2:22 NASB

Temptations? Run!

Temptations all share one thing in common: They can be lethal to our faith. The more we give in to small temptations, the easier it becomes to excuse away the "biggies" when they face us down. Over time, the soul erosion steals our joy and saps our spiritual energy. We long for serenity.

The prayer of Jabez in 1 Chronicles 4:10 asks God not only to *deliver* him from evil but to *preserve* him from it. Preservation means never entering the arena of temptation in the first place. But when temptations do come knocking—as they surely will—the best form of defense is to run far and fast. If we refuse to entertain temptation, it holds no power over us.

Are you facing temptations right now? Ask God to put a "fence" around you—spirit, soul, and body. And don't open the gate.

Be on guard for temptations,
refusing to play the game.

Motivation is when
your dreams put
on work clothes.

*Whatever you do, work at it
with all your heart, as working
for the Lord, not for men.*

COLOSSIANS 3:23 NIV

Make Your Dream Come True!

Maybe you've heard the expression "putting feet to your prayers." In the same way, our dreams need the true grit that comes from motivation—a stick-to-it-iveness that lifts them out of the realm of "could be" and moves them toward reality. Propelled by the feet of motivation, dreams have a way of coming true.

Do you need some fuel to get your motivation fires burning again?

- Ask for God's favor and direction as you pursue your dream.

- Tell a trusted friend your dream. Give her periodic progress reports.

- Write out your dream and the steps (within your power) to bring it to fruition.

- Post a picture or brief description of your dream/goal in a place where you will see it often—such as on the bathroom mirror, refrigerator door, computer terminal, or car visor.

Dream big, listen long, and work hard!

Death is not a period
but a comma in the
story of one's life.

Jesus said unto her [Martha],
I am the resurrection, and the life:
he that believeth in me, though he
were dead, yet shall he live:
And whosoever liveth and
believeth in me shall never die.

JOHN 11:25-26

The Rest of Your Story?

We may forget at times, but our lives really are magnificent tales written by the hand of God, full of plot twists and turns. Some are not to our liking; others surprise us with joy. But until we reach the vantage point of eternity, we will not be able to see the full story. Only then, when we no longer "see through a glass darkly," will every puzzle piece fall into place and every "coincidence" reveal its meaning.

Even then the story goes on.

Our finite minds boggle at the thought of all those endless hours in eternity, but God promises that life with Him will surpass our wildest dreams. Your personal story, which God began on the day in which you were conceived, doesn't end when you step into eternity. It merely starts a new chapter, more exciting than the last.

Remember that you are the lead character in a very personal story. Make it count.

A pint of example is worth
a barrelful of advice.

*Join in following my example, and
observe those who walk according
to the pattern you have in us.*

PHILIPPIANS 3:17 NASB

Living Your Words

It's tempting to offer advice when we're *sure* we know what's best for someone. But unless asked for, advice is often better left unsaid. We have good intentions, but advice often loses its graciousness the moment it leaves our lips. Think of times when a friend or relative offered "helpful hints" that you never wanted to hear.

A life well lived, on the other hand, is the best teacher there is. It speaks louder than any words could ever shout. And when it comes to living out one's faith, the best barometer of a godly life is the daily interactions that reveal the heart.

As you go about your business today, remember that people are watching you—not just the physical you, but your attitude, your speech, your actions, and your temperament. What unspoken advice will you offer today?

Make it a goal to live what you believe today.

Every person should have
a fair-sized cemetery
in which to bury
the faults of friends.

Be ye kind one to another,
tenderhearted, forgiving
one another, even as God for
Christ's sake hath forgiven you.

EPHESIANS 4:32

Passing on God's Kindness

A friend or loved one goofs up, and what do we do? We're tempted to rub their noses in it as we see their faults in glaring neon lights. Our own faults seem so, well, *excusable* in comparison. But a life of faith is lived on a higher plane than the one ordered by human nature. God calls us up to a higher place.

He calls us to forgiveness, the cornerstone of grace because Someone forgave us first. Remember the old saying "pretty is as pretty does"? Kindness is a trait that's only as good as its practice. A tender heart extends grace even when people don't deserve it, like God did when He sent Jesus to die while we were yet sinners.

Count it a privilege to be kind to others, to treat them tenderly, and to forgive them when no one else will. Be like the One you follow.

Sprinkle your day with a heavy dose of kindness.

Life is not a problem
to be solved but a
gift to be enjoyed.

*This is the day the
LORD has made; let us
rejoice and be glad in it.*

PSALM 118:24 NIV

Piecing Together the Big Picture of Life

Remember your first jigsaw puzzle, the overwhelming task of putting it together? According to the picture on the box, all those oddly shaped pieces would somehow—miraculously—form a single image, a coherent whole. You struggled with pieces only to find they didn't seem to fit together.

But then something wonderful happened. Two pieces finally matched, and then a third, and a fourth. Your enthusiasm for the puzzle increased with every piece that fell into place. And, sure enough, a picture emerged, just as the box cover promised. You couldn't wait for the next puzzle.

Life can be fraught with struggles at times, but we can stop to remember that it all will make sense in time. As the pieces fit together, life becomes an adventure, a joyful journey whose own unique image will fully emerge someday.

Today is an important piece of the whole picture of your life.

Faith does not mean believing
without evidence. It means
believing in realities that go
beyond sense and sight—for
which a totally different
sort of evidence is required.

*We look not at the things which are seen,
but at the things which are not seen: for
the things which are seen are temporal; but
the things which are not seen are eternal.*

2 CORINTHIANS 4:18

Trust Me!

Missourians carry a proud motto on their license plates: "The Show-Me State." Not ones for having the wool pulled over their eyes, they value the time-tested standard of believing something only after they've seen it. In the face of such common sense, what God asks of us seems risky. "Trust Me," He says. "Have faith in Me." Yet God remains invisible to our finite eyes, and the things He promises—well, we prefer hard evidence, thank you very much.

The apostle Paul, however, penned words that resonate deep within our spirits: "I know whom I have believed, and am persuaded." Faith doesn't make sense to us. But when we take the plunge, we discover that He really is always faithful. He is prepared to show us His goodness and mercy and His perfect plan for our lives.

*Trust God with something small today,
and watch your faith grow.*

Kindness is the oil
that takes the
friction out of life.

*The fruit of the Spirit is . . .
kindness.*

GALATIANS 5:22 NIV

The Oil of Kindness

A door with squeaky hinges grates on the metal— and everyone's nerves. But add a little spray lubricant, and the irritating squawk goes away. Once it's oiled, the door functions properly and pleasantly. All it takes is a little grease.

Life and other people have a way of grating on our nerves, too, sometimes, but we can smooth things over with the oil of kindness. Like lubricant for the soul, kindness quiets our tempers and keeps friction to a minimum, lessening the chances for sparks to fly when we're rubbed the wrong way.

The next time something tests your patience or threatens your calm, stop and "oil" the situation with kindness. Ask God to apply His Spirit to the situation, working through you when you've exhausted your own resources. You, and all those involved, will appreciate the difference He makes.

Don't leave the house until you've given your spirit an "oil change"!

Ninety percent of the
friction of daily life
is caused by the
wrong tone of voice.

*When you talk, you should
always be kind and wise.
Then you will be able to answer
everyone in the way you should.*

COLOSSIANS 4:6 NCV

Not Just What—How!

Did you know that *how* you say something can carry as much weight as *what* you say? Think about it this way: A mother cuddles her toddler and says, "You've been a bad boy." But she grins as she says the words, and he hears the loving tone, the teasing inflection, in her voice. He laps up her words because they are laced with love. But if the same mother says sharply, "You've been a bad boy!" the child hears the anger in her voice, sees her frowning face, and deduces that he's in trouble. The same words–opposite meanings.

Though certain times call for different inflections, words "seasoned with salt" and mellowed by a loving tone pave the way for good communication and right relationships. Your voice is a powerful tool. Use it wisely!

Keep the bite out of your "bark" at all times.

You should never let
adversity get you down—
except on your knees.

*I am persuaded, that neither death,
nor life, nor angels, nor principalities,
nor powers, nor things present, nor
things to come . . . shall be able to
separate us from the love of God,
which is in Christ Jesus our Lord.*

ROMANS 8:38-39

Facing Adversity

For most of us, the pattern is unmistakable: the moment adversity strikes, we fall to our knees and beg God to lighten the load—or change the circumstances altogether. We pound on Heaven's door until we get an answer to our desperate plea. And somehow with the answer comes growth.

Hard times are a part of life, but we can grow by experiencing them. When we allow dark seasons to drive us to our knees, we discover we aren't wading through the valley alone. God is there beside us every step of the way, awakening our faith, strengthening our resolve, and lifting our spirit. He is always faithful.

A life lived in tandem with God doesn't buy you insurance from pain and sorrow. But it does guarantee that you will emerge from the trial a better person than you were before.

Take God's hand before stepping out your door today.

It's the little things
in life that determine
the big things.

Thou hast been faithful over
a few things, I will make thee
ruler over many things: enter
thou into the joy of thy lord.

MATTHEW 25:21

The Little Things

Taking time for the little things may seem like stepping into a bog when you have mountains to climb. Frustrated, you slog your way through and press onward, sure that the mountains are where true satisfaction lies. But God's economy uses the currency of little things. Only by sweating through the "bog" of small things are we made ready for the really big stuff when it comes along. The lowlands hone our character and fit us for the summit.

As you go through your day, make a conscious decision to appreciate those little things. Think back on some goal you accomplished, and recall the many small steps that led you there. Seen in this light, small things become sacred moments—stepping stones that pave the way to your dreams coming true.

Relish the small things in your life today.

To know the will of God is
the greatest knowledge.
To find the will of God is
the greatest discovery. But
to do the will of God is the
greatest achievement.

If anyone serves Me, he must continue to
follow Me [to cleave steadfastly to
Me, conform wholly to My example
in living . . .] and wherever I am, there
will My servant be also. If anyone
serves Me, the Father will honor him.

JOHN 12:26 AMP

Real Knowledge

Self-knowledge and self-will are trumpeted as worthy goals in the game of life. "Knowledge is power," we hear people say. Therefore, knowing yourself must be the cornerstone of power, the basis for future growth. A dogged determination to clamber up the ladder of success goes hand in hand with the gaining of knowledge. Clinch the deal in both categories, and you find happiness. Or so the thinking goes.

Not surprisingly, God's plan for human lives cuts across this popular dogma. He tells us in unwavering terms that a holy awe for Him is the beginning of wisdom, the cornerstone of knowledge. Following His lead takes more boldness than following the crowd. Those who believe in Him discover that the most exciting life was waiting for them all along. They only needed to hear God's voice and then heed it.

Following God is better than
following the crowd.

Nothing beats love
at first sight except
love with insight.

The beginning of wisdom is this:
Get wisdom, and whatever
else you get, get insight.

PROVERBS 4:7 NRSV

Love with Eyes Wide Open

The old saying "Love is blind" is true. When we're in love, we see our beloved's strengths, not his weaknesses. And even if we acknowledge the weak points, we usually excuse them. This blind infatuation feels good, but even better is true love with our eyes wide open—love that sees all and yet chooses to love.

Unconditional love is one of those quiet qualities of love that doesn't get a lot of media attention. Extreme love, puppy love, unrequited love, forbidden love, love at first sight—they all get their heyday in the pop culture of song lyrics, movie themes, and book plots. But when was the last time you heard someone talk about love that sees the good, the bad, and the ugly and yet keeps on loving?

Loving is rigorous work. It calls us to love in spite of circumstances and to put others before self. It's grown-up love—true love.

*Love without limits today,
one moment at a time.*

It is cheaper to pardon
than to resent. Forgiveness
saves the expense of anger,
the cost of hatred.

*If ye forgive men their trespasses,
your heavenly Father will also
forgive you: But if ye forgive not
men their trespasses, neither will
your Father forgive your trespasses.*

MATTHEW 6:14-15

Setting Yourself Free

A black bear paced the length of its cage, back and forth, every day for years. As the faces of zoo-goers peered through the bars, the bear ambled along its solitary path, miserable.

One day the zookeeper retired the bear to a forest preserve, but the men who hauled the bear to the preserve noticed something peculiar: Having acres to roam, the bear paced back and forth in a ten-by-eight-foot pattern, day in and day out. The forest was there, but the bear never could enjoy it.

The habit of unforgiveness cages us as well. The moment we choose to forgive, it's as if we unlock fetters that have held us in a lethal grip. For anger is lethal to our health, both spiritually and physically. If we do nothing else today, we need to forgive one person who has hurt us. Then we in turn will be healed.

Forgive and escape the high cost of hatred.

Be like a postage stamp—
stick to one thing
till you get there.

Be steadfast, immovable, always
abounding in the work of the
Lord, knowing that your toil
is not in vain in the Lord.

1 CORINTHIANS 15:58 NASB

A Cure for Dreamer's Block

Have you ever felt so overwhelmed by a to-do list that you wound up getting nothing done? The dozens of tasks all scream for attention, drowning out your ability to think clearly, much less perform them in an efficient manner.

One remedy for this "worker's block" is to shorten your list to two or three critical tasks–things you *have* to accomplish in a given day. By tackling a few items at a time, the list becomes manageable, and your sanity is saved.

This technique works on a larger scale too. Several dreams may be vying for attention within your spirit. By focusing on one or two biggies–the "must" dreams– you improve your chances of achieving them. Like adhesive on a stamp, you'll find that the dreams you hold on to tenaciously won't let *you* go either.

Dream big dreams, and follow
them with all your heart.

I have held many things in
my hands and lost them
all; but the things I have
placed in God's hands,
those I always possess.

I know whom I have believed,
and am persuaded that he is able to
keep that which I have committed
unto him against that day.

2 TIMOTHY 1:12

Lose to Gain!

The temptation to "count your chickens before they're hatched" loses its fizzle when you've discovered, once too often, that unhatched eggs never strut around the farmyard. It's much better to wait and see a dream hatched with God's blessing than to try to force it into fruition on our own. One way leads to a life of fulfillment, the other only to frustration.

We long to grasp things, to stake our claim to them. But, like so many other divine paradoxes, we often find that only when we let things go—give them to God—do they become truly ours. In losing, we gain.

It sounds like a cliché, but practice letting go and letting God today. In the end, you only possess what you let Him have anyway. And He wants to give you much more than that.

Give your dreams to God. He'll do the rest.

Nothing is so strong as gentleness. Nothing is so gentle as real strength.

You have also given me the shield of Your salvation, And Your right hand upholds me; And Your gentleness makes me great.

PSALM 18:35 NASB

The God Kind of Strength

Gentle strength is one of those perplexing traits that sets a person apart from the pack. We may at first be fooled by gentleness, which can be mistaken for weakness. Gentle strength is the God kind of strength. It's His nature at work in human hearts. Gentleness without strength can leave a person vulnerable. Strength without gentleness may result in brute force. But when the two are combined, the result is a Godly meekness, a strong serenity.

The psalmist praised the gentleness of God for making him great. That's another way of saying that God's quiet Spirit within us makes us valiant in whatever tasks we undertake with Him. When God goes with us—and works through us—a watching world is left in awe. They witness gentle strength in action and wonder, *What's their secret?*

Let your strength be laced with gentleness.

People may doubt
what you say, but they
will always believe
what you do.

*The tree is known and recognized
and judged by its fruit.*

MATTHEW 12:33 AMP

Hypocrisy at Fifty Paces?

"Your actions speak so loud I can't hear what you're saying!"

This saying gets our attention because it's so true. What we say is not nearly as meaningful as what we do. Children know this instinctively. Their razor-sharp perceptions pick up hypocrisy at fifty paces. We might be able to fool other adults, but we can't fool children. They see through facades to the true nature hiding behind. How much better it would be never to wear those masks at all.

Just as an apple tree always bears apples, not persimmons, we always bear the fruit that's in our hearts. A heart rooted in love responds with loving actions. A heart rooted in deceit hides behind ulterior motives.

Let people come to know you by your "fruit," and let that fruit always be the Godly kind.

*Let your actions speak loudly
of God's love today.*

The trouble with
stretching the truth is
that it's apt to snap back.

*A false witness shall not
be unpunished, and he that
speaketh lies shall not escape.*

PROVERBS 19:5

Lies Boomerang!

We scold children for lying, yet we often sugarcoat the truth ourselves—or just bend it a little. But truth doesn't need garnishing, and bending it only makes it into a boomerang. Deceit speaks out of one side of the mouth and cuts corners to achieve results. Truth speaks for itself and wins out in the end.

Whenever you're tempted to tell a "white lie," remember that little choices are the means by which character is made. Every time you choose to speak the truth, to follow the rules, to abide by the law, you show off the character of God within you. Even if no one else knows you're stretching the truth, He does—and so do you.

Make it a goal in your life always to speak the truth, no matter the cost. Ultimately, a life of truthfulness pays high dividends.

Tell the truth, and it won't tell on you.

Mirth is God's medicine.
Everybody ought to bathe
in it. Grim care, moroseness,
anxiety—all this rust of life
ought to be scoured
off by the oil of mirth.

*A happy heart is good medicine and
a cheerful mind works healing, but a
broken spirit dries up the bones.*

PROVERBS 17:22 AMP

Catch the Bug! Laugh!

A good belly laugh is a speedy cure for a drooping spirit. Someone once said laughter is the music of the soul. If that's true, then "sing" as often as you can. Look for the humorous in life. Find the funny in every situation—even when it looks sour on the outside.

God must have known our spirits would need recharging on a regular basis. In addition to time with Him and the companionship of friends, He has provided us with the release that comes from laughter bubbling up from our spirits.

Here's a good primer for the laughter-impaired: Go to a playground, sit on a bench, and watch children play for thirty minutes. Notice how often they laugh, simply with the joy of being alive. Watch them until their laughter becomes infectious, and make sure you catch that "bug."

Take a hearty draught of
"merry medicine" today.

The right train of
thought can take you to
a better station in life.

*As he thinks within himself,
so he is.*

PROVERBS 23:7 NASB

Think and Be!

The pop psychology called "positive thinking" came on the scene in the 1980s, selling thousands of books and tapes, turning its leading practitioners into millionaires. "Think good things, and those things will happen to you," they said. Stay positive in your mind, and life will roll out the red carpet. Though excessive at times, this belief system isn't very far from the truth. And the pop-psych gurus of the 1980s can't take all the credit.

God is the original author of positive thinking. Proverbs states His final word on the matter: "As he thinks within himself, so he is." Just as our words contain power, so our thoughts do also. And when we allow God to shape our thoughts, they lead to lives that line up with His will. There's no more positive way to live than that.

Remember that the One who created the world has your best interests at heart.

You cannot do a kindness
too soon, because you
never know how soon
it will be too late!

*Encourage one another day
after day, as long as it is
still called "Today."*

HEBREWS 3:13 NASB

Doing the Unexpected— Kindness!

Do you remember a time when a stranger surprised you with an unexpected kindness? Perhaps the individual picked up a fallen package when your arms were full. Maybe another driver let you into traffic, at risk of missing the light change. Or perhaps a shopper allowed you to check out first, so you could get home with your screaming baby.

Kindness costs so little but means so much. And since we don't know what tomorrow holds, this is the best day to practice your kindness skills on others. It doesn't take much time out of your day to hold a door, pick up stray garbage at the curb, or smile at your grouchy neighbor.

You may lift someone's spirit or make it possible for a person to make it through a very difficult time just by your shedding a little light on another's path.

Sow good seeds today and harvest them tomorrow.

Do you wish to be great?
Then begin by
being humble.

*A man's pride shall bring
him low: but honour shall
uphold the humble in spirit.*

PROVERBS 29:23

Forgetting What You're Up To

Our culture is tainted with a what's-in-it-for-me attitude. Everywhere we look we see signs of selfishness. The "Me Generation" mentality spawned out of the '80s pervades everyday life. No wonder it's so refreshing when we stumble onto genuine humility—when people quietly go about the business God called them to, making sure He gets the credit.

One of the Bible's overlooked treasures is this simple teaching: when you do good deeds, don't let your right hand know what the left hand is doing. In other words, be so concerned with doing good—not with getting the credit—that you forget what you're up to. When you are focused on helping others, rather than tooting your own horn, the blessing comes back to you, sometimes in surprising ways. God promises the life of humility and honor will always be rewarded.

Take the high road, and you'll never find yourself in the lowlands.

It isn't hard to make a mountain out of a molehill. Just add a little dirt.

Starting a quarrel is like breaching a dam; so drop the matter before a dispute breaks out.

PROVERBS 17:14 NIV

Keeping the Peace

At heated moments, having our say seems critical. But later, we may wonder why we didn't just keep our mouths shut. Being right or being the last one to speak isn't very rewarding in the long run—or even in the short run. But preserving a relationship is.

Remember the story of the boy with his finger stuck in a dike? That one small finger held back water that, if loosed, would have toppled the wall and flooded a town. Like rushing water, an argument can rage out of control, ruining everything in its wake. But when we choose to forgive and calmly resolve a matter or drop it altogether, it's like plugging the dike with our finger. In that one small action we accomplish something big: keeping peace with a friend or loved one.

Keep the molehill from becoming a mountain; drop your dirt.

An argument avoided is a friendship saved.

Conscience is God's built-in warning system. Be very happy when it hurts you. Be very worried when it doesn't.

I strive always to keep my conscience clear before God and man.

ACTS 24:16 NIV

Your Natural Alarm System

Houses wired with alarm systems have an extra barrier of protection against intrusion. If someone tries to break into such a house, sirens blare or a silent signal is sent to the police. Most would-be burglars bypass houses with security system signs posted in the yard. Why go through the hassle and risk getting caught?

God installs His moral code into every human heart at birth, but it's our job to keep that internal alarm system working. When we do something wrong, the sirens go off. But if we hear the warning bells and continually ignore them, eventually they won't ring anymore. We lose the sensitivity God intended for us to have.

A life that's tuned to God's voice remains supple and sensitive—capable of being shaped by the Potter's hands. Never forget that a nagging conscience is a blessing.

Whenever your conscience speaks, pay close attention!

Give your troubles
to God: He will be up
all night anyway.

He will not allow your foot
to slip; He who keeps
you will not slumber.

PSALM 121:3 NASB

Trouble Sleeping?

No one likes to burn the midnight oil after a long day's work—no one but God, that is. He's always on call, ready to answer our cries in the dark. But when troubles weigh on us heavily, our minds spin; we analyze, trying to sort things out; we consider choices, and our nerves get tangled into a knot. At last we sleep but wake up tired the next morning.

What a miserable way to live! Yet we easily slip into this pattern unless we remember that God never sleeps and He longs to carry our troubles for us. The psalmist said that God "keeps" us. That word evokes the image of a shepherd keeping watch over a flock of sheep. The sheep don't worry; it's the shepherd's job to take care of things and to keep the sheep safe from harm.

When troubles steal your sleep,
give your troubles to God.

The best way to get the
last word is to apologize.

*If you have been trapped by what
you said, ensnared by the words
of your mouth, then do this, my
son, to free yourself, since you have
fallen into your neighbor's hands:
Go and humble yourself; press
your plea with your neighbor!*

PROVERBS 6:2-3 NIV

"I'm Sorry"

These two little words hold incredible power. They can smooth out kinks in strained relationships and restore goodwill before anger moves in. The moment we utter these words, we open the door for healing to take place. Apologizing may look weak, but it is amazing how much strength it takes to do it. Yet often we are the ones who benefit the most. And it all starts with lowering our pride and saying those words.

Has someone hurt you? Have you wronged another? Why not be the instigator of forgiveness, and watch what happens. Even if you're not at fault, saying "I'm sorry" could make all the difference in saving a friendship.

Try this experiment: every time you say something you shouldn't have or you do something wrong this week, apologize on the spot. Don't wait. With practice, it will become a habit.

Saying "I'm sorry" is a sign
of strength, not weakness.

I dare not choose my lot;
I would not if I might.
Choose thou for me, my
God, So shall I walk aright.

*Blessed be the Lord, who
daily loadeth us with benefits,
even the God of our salvation.*

When No Is Good

It's been said that when life's disappointments come, remember that a no from God only means He wants the best for you. In fact, He wants it so much that He is willing to see you disappointed today in order to give you His best tomorrow. Armed with that knowledge, we can face disappointments with a new perspective, waiting in quiet anticipation for the "best" that God has for us.

We may plot and scheme, but the outcome of our dreams and lives is up to God. Our meddling will only frustrate His perfect plan. Our interruptions get us off track and delay the fulfillment of what lies in store.

God's best often means leaving behind what is merely good. Hold your desires with a light grip, ready to let go, and wait for His best. It will be well worth it.

*Waiting is easy when you know
the end is worthwhile.*

Small numbers make
no difference to God.
There is nothing
small if God is in it.

*Be strong and courageous, and act;
do not fear nor be dismayed, for the
LORD God, my God, is with you.*

1 CHRONICLES 28:20 NASB

Shoot for the Moon!

For Walt Disney, it all started with a mouse. How did your dream begin? Has anything slowed it down?

Fear is perhaps the greatest enemy of dreaming. Dreams take shape in our spirits. Our passion fuels them. We pursue our dreams, taking steps to make them come true. Then a problem crashes onto the scene, like a fallen tree blocking a roadway. The problem seems insurmountable; the fear of failure keeps us from plunging into the unknown, so we hang back on the shore where it's safe—but void of dreams.

God put the capacity to dream into our spirits, so He must have intended for us to use this ability. Someone once said, "Shoot for the moon; you may hit the treetops." God may wish us to aim for—and expect to hit—the moon in the first place!

Remember that a big God is on your side.

The best antique
is an old friend.

Your own friend and your father's
friend, forsake them not . . .
Better is a neighbor who is near
[in spirit] than a brother
who is far off [in heart].

PROVERBS 27:10 AMP

Old Friends

There in the back corner of the shop you spot it—the armoire you've been looking for. You move closer for a good look and notice its intricate detail and skilled carving. The price tag is too good to be true, so you buy it. Once home, you realize the armoire is a rare antique—a wardrobe generations old—and valuable because of it.

Like antiques, old friends are rare and of great value, and we are blessed when we have them in our lives. New friends may come and go, but the old friends stand the test of time and distance. They're the ones who remember our birthdays. They're the ones who let us call in the middle of the night if needed, who keep taking us back, no matter how many times we goof up.

Old friends are a gift from God.

Call a lifelong friend today and thank her for her love.

A day hemmed in prayer
is less likely to unravel.

Pray about everything; tell God your needs, and don't forget to thank him for his answers. If you do this, you will experience God's peace . . . His peace will keep your thoughts and your hearts quiet and at rest.

PHILIPPIANS 4:6-7 TLB

Hemming Your Day

Ask anyone who sews, and they'll tell you how important a hem is. Without a hem, the fabric will fray. Or try crocheting without tying off the last stitch. One pull on the yarn, and the whole thing unravels. What started as, say, an afghan ends up as a ball of curly yarn.

Prayer is like the hem of a garment, there to secure the edges and protect the inner fabric. It keeps us from unraveling throughout the day and reminds us that we're here for a purpose. Prayer gives meaning to each day. It's like an instant messenger system to God when we're frightened or worried or stressed—or simply wanting to talk to Him.

Start today with a prayer, and "tie off" the hem before you lay your head down tonight. The result will be a day full of peace.

Tell God what's on your heart.
He's always listening.

God never asks about our
ability or our inability—
just our availability.

*I heard the voice of the Lord,
saying, Whom shall I send, and
who will go for us? Then said I,
Here am I; send me.*

ISAIAH 6:8

Who Will Go for Us?

Suppose you're standing in the rain in a foreign city, trying to hail a cab. At that moment, the best taxi driver isn't the one most skillful behind the wheel; it's the one who stops to pick you up. In that desperate situation, availability is all that matters. You plunge into the taxi's dry interior and whisper a prayer of thanks—somebody was there for you.

God doesn't care how smart we are or how many stomach crunches we can pull off. He doesn't search for good looks or a hip personality. The main thing that matters to Him is availability. Are we willing to go where He says? Are we prepared to do whatever He asks? Do we have the faith to follow in the dark?

Make yourself available to God, and He'll give you a life of adventure.

Be there! And be ready to go!

Fair words never
hurt the tongue.

Pleasant words are a honeycomb,
Sweet to the soul and
healing to the bones.

PROVERBS 16:24 NASB

Brighten Someone's Day

You have the ability to brighten someone's day with a word. You hold the key to making them smile, to erasing sadness and giving them hope. You can boost confidence or destroy it. You can hurt or heal. Your words, so intangible, are anything but meaningless. Think of how God created the world. What medium did He choose? The spoken word. Yet we forget that our own words contain power.

Make it a goal to say kind words to everyone today. Watch for their reactions. Take note of the words others say, and note how those words make you feel. When you realize the full potential bound up in words, you may never talk the same way again. Speak as if every person you interact with were a dear friend. In God's eyes, they are just that special.

Let your words be full of grace today!

Forget yourself for others, and others will not forget you!

"In everything, do to others what you would have them do to you, for this sums up the Law and the Prophets."

MATTHEW 7:12 NIV

The Golden Code

Remember when your mother told you about the Golden Rule? It was not only good advice, it was "God" advice—treat others the way you want to be treated yourself. Do for them what you'd like done for you. Remember others and forget about yourself. Those who live by this golden code find the secret to lifelong blessing, because good deeds sown today reap a harvest tomorrow.

As you go about your day, find ways to "do unto others" until Golden-Rule behavior is second nature to you. Watch for clues to what would help others. Then act accordingly.

It's true that when we hoard things—including acts of kindness—we often lose them in the end. But the moment we open the floodgates and give without reserve, God opens the floodgates of Heaven to us. Give like you mean it!

Be concerned with others more than yourself.

Everyone has patience.
Successful people
learn to use it.

Let patience have her perfect
work, that ye may be perfect
and entire, wanting nothing.

JAMES 1:4

Wait a Minute!

We're conditioned to be in a hurry. The microwave dinner takes one minute longer to cook, and we sigh. We tap our foot when the line at the video store winds like a theme-park queue, adding fifteen minutes to the trip. Our Internet connection seems adequate until we sample high-speed access.

Everything in today's culture screams, "Get it now!" From instant access banking to drive-through weddings, tasks that once took hours are now reduced to minutes—sometimes even seconds. Still our patience wears thin. Bottom line? We still need patience.

Training your patience is like learning to ride a bike. The first few times you try it, everything feels wobbly and out of synch. But after a few wipeouts, you get the hang of it. And as a bonus, patience will smooth your way and that of others through each day.

Deliberately slow your pace today.
Waiting can be wonderful!

The secret of contentment
is the realization that
life is a gift, not a right.

*Godliness with contentment is
great gain. For we brought
nothing into this world, and it is
certain we can carry nothing out.*

1 TIMOTHY 6:6-7

The Gift of Today

When you woke up this morning, what went through your head? Did you realize the new day was a gift? The moment we take the sunrise for granted, we begin the slow slide toward indifference and ingratitude. Soon we take people for granted and, worst of all, even God. We may come to expect His goodness as our right, but it is not. It is a gift—a precious gift.

Whenever obligation is attached to gift giving, gifts lose their meaning. Suddenly the joy goes out of giving and receiving. But give—or receive—a gift unexpectedly, and something remarkable takes place. Joy lights a face. Eyes and hearts connect. Gratitude binds two people.

None of us is guaranteed tomorrow—only this moment. When you realize every day is a gift, it increases the value of everything.

*Be content with what today offers;
treasure it as if it were your last.*

Honesty is the first
chapter of the book
of wisdom.

*Provide things honest in
the sight of all men.*

ROMANS 12:17

Honesty Is Good Thinking

Honesty is wisdom. Now there's a profound thought. Consider adding a twist to it: when people open up the "book" of your life, let honesty be the *first* chapter they read. All the other chapters of your life will fall into their proper sequence when the first one is in place. When you start with honesty, you move toward a high conclusion. Your story ends well—no matter what happens in the pages between.

Honesty is one of those underrated values that is taken for granted until it's gone. Its absence may go unnoticed until you look for it. But when it's present in a life, it shines like a polished gemstone, adorning the bearer with beauty and grace.

Keep the plain, simple truth as your banner. It will serve you well—to the very last page of the book.

Choose truth, not consequences.

The art of being wise
is the art of knowing
what to overlook.

A man's wisdom gives him
patience; it is to his glory
to overlook an offense.

PROVERBS 19:11 NIV

Overlooking an Offense—Glory!

A gracious spirit is one that notices the good things in people and overlooks the bad. Proverbs uses powerful language to describe this trait: it is to a person's glory to "overlook an offense" in another. Glory suggests much more than mere goodness. It touches on the supernatural—that part of a human being that will live forever. God bottles our tears; maybe He keeps an accounting of our moments of glory also.

It's tempting to read a laundry list of personal faults when someone angers you. You may want to lash out, reminding the individual of the error. But when you find yourself faced with that situation, stop and see the person through God's eyes—eyes of grace, eyes of potential, eyes that see who the person could be. Do so, and you will have committed an act of glory.

Train your eyes to look for the good and overlook the bad in others.

The best way to hold
a man is in your arms.

The man should give his wife all
that is her right as a married
woman, and the wife should
do the same for her husband.

1 CORINTHIANS 7:3 TLB

Hold Your Spouse

The longing for love runs deep within us. Love of family and friends keeps us steady; but the love between a man and a woman occupies a place in our hearts like no other. A tender well of emotion, it fills us and completes us—making us better people than we were before. Romantic love claims us body, soul, and spirit, involving the whole of our being. No wonder God compares the love between a man and a woman with His own love for us.

Has God blessed you with the love of a man? If so, treasure that love (and that person). It is a gift. "Hugs" from God are good for the soul, but there's nothing like hugging someone with skin on.

Treasure the one you love in your heart, but hold them in your arms as well.

*Open your arms and your heart
to the one you love.*

The only way to have
a friend is to be one.

*A man that hath friends must
shew himself friendly.*

PROVERBS 18:24

True Friendship

Making friends is one of life's sweetest pleasures; keeping them for a lifetime is sublime. Friends make the journey of life worth traveling. They keep us humble when we could easily turn prideful, and they encourage us when we droop. True friends remind us of our best qualities and overlook our worst. A real friend knows the real you and sticks around anyway.

Remember how it felt to make your first friend? Maybe you were on the swing set or playing in the sandbox. Another boy or girl started playing beside you, and before long you were laughing together. When you ran home, you couldn't wait to go out and play again—you had a friend.

Acquaintances come and go, but true friendship is forever. Make it your goal to be the kind of friend that "sticketh closer than a brother."

Be a person who's known for being a true friend.

God can heal a broken
heart, but He has to
have all the pieces.

My child, give me your heart.

PROVERBS 23:26 NRSV

More Room in a Broken Heart

We may see heartache's approach or be caught by surprise when it hits. Either way, we are left devastated in its wake, feeling as if our hearts have been shattered into pieces or crushed flat.

Then, for some, comes the task of building a wall of protection to prevent being hurt again. Brick by brick many build a fortress around their hearts thinking they'll be safe, but they only shut themselves in, cutting themselves off from love.

Is your heart broken? Resist the temptation to build walls; let God rebuild your life instead. Take a bigger risk. Give Him permission to take your heart completely so that He can remold it into something supple and new. A line from an old pop song had it right: there is more room in a broken heart—more room to love again.

*Let God make more room
for love in your heart.*

Do not follow where
the path may lead—
go instead where there is
no path and leave a trail.

*Your ears shall hear a
word behind you, saying,
"This is the way, walk in it."*

ISAIAH 30:21 NKJV

Blazing a Spiritual Trail

Trailblazing is hard work. With no path to follow, you hack your way through thick foliage and move at a snail's pace. It's much easier to follow a trail that's already there, a foot-worn path clearly marked through the woods. The only hitch is that you're heading down a trail someone else blazed—which may or may not lead to where you want to go. Making your own path results in a sure destination and the satisfaction of knowing you didn't settle for a route just because it was easy.

Look around you. Most people follow the well-worn path with the rest of the herd, don't they? In contrast, those who live by faith seem to walk a different path—narrow and difficult at times, but wildly fruitful.

Don't settle. Listen for God's direction, and blaze a trail where He leads you to go.

Take the road less traveled
and reap rich rewards.

I regret often that
I have spoken; never
that I have been silent.

In the multitude of words there
wanteth not sin: but he that
refraineth his lips is wise.

PROVERBS 10:19

God's Words

A lot of words can lead to a lot of problems, but keeping silent almost never does. Isn't it odd how such a small thing—the tongue—can wag beyond all proportion and wreak havoc in a life? Sometimes not just our lives get bent out of shape by what we say; those around us can feel the sting of our words, too, yet we can never take them back.

What you say can make all the difference over a lifetime. Barbed words lead to strained relationships and bitterness. Gentle words pave the way for love to work its healing touch on you and on those you encounter.

Ask God to fill you with words He would say as you meet each person on your way. Practice kindness in your speech, and you will reap it in your relationships.

You catch more bees with honey than with vinegar.

Some people complain
because God put thorns on
roses, while others praise Him
for putting roses among thorns.

*Whatsoever things are true, whatsoever
things are honest, whatsoever things
are just, whatsoever things are pure,
whatsoever things are lovely, whatsoever
things are of good report; if there
be any virtue, and if there be any
praise, think on these things.*

PHILIPPIANS 4:8

Illuminating Dark Days

Many of us do not like cloudy days, and we long for the sunshine. We also dislike those dark days when physical or emotional hurt paints the day in somber shades.

A child once asked a painter why he used so many dark colors in a portrait. He explained that the darkness was necessary to make the light more radiant; he needed shadows to show off the bright features. The finished work, a portrait of rare beauty, was known for its look of illumination, as if someone had shone a light on the face while the artist worked. Everyone marveled at the portrait's brightness. They never noticed the dark hues that intensified it.

A Master Painter is at work amongst your shadows as well. Let them bring attention to His handiwork in your life. Let them point to the glory of God.

Even bad things are used for our good in the hands of God.

The voice of parents is the voice of gods, for to their children they are heaven's lieutenants.

Teach them [God's commandments] to your children, talking about them when you sit at home and when you walk along the road, when you lie down and when you get up . . . So that your days and the days of your children may be many.

DEUTERONOMY 11:19, 21 NIV

Children—A Sacred Trust

The Bible says that children are a blessing from the Lord. If we're honest, they often seem like nuisances—small packages that wield great power and wreak havoc. They scream and fight with each other; they trash the house and demand to be fed every couple of hours. Yet God calls them a blessing!

It's easy to love a child who loves you back. The struggle comes when that growing person plays a love-hate game with your emotions. If you're struggling to recall the warm fuzzies your children once evoked, remember that you are not too different from your children in God's eyes. Yet He loves you even when you're challenging—even when you reject Him.

One of the hardest tasks ever, raising children is a job of the highest caliber. And just think—God chose *you* for the job!

God has entrusted precious gifts to you;
treat them with utmost care.

Silence is deep
as eternity. Speech is
shallow as time.

*To every thing there is a season,
and a time to every purpose under
the heaven . . . a time to keep
silence, and a time to speak.*

ECCLESIASTES 3:1, 7

Listen to the Silence

Silence, like solitude, is an underrated treasure in this hectic world. We fill our days with endless activity and get bombarded with noise at every turn. We chatter away when the best choice would be to listen. We wear headphones when we might hear birds instead. When was the last time you sat down in the quiet and simply listened to the silence?

Do you allow silence inside your spirit? Many drown out the voice of God with endless activity and noise. One old saint made it a point to spend one day a month sitting out somewhere in nature. Sometime during that day, God would say something, and this sincere seeker was quiet enough to hear what He said. Too busy for a whole day? Take a moment then. Look out your window and listen for His voice.

Become rich by storing up "golden silence."

Action is eloquence;
the eyes of the ignorant
are more learned
than their ears.

My son, forget not my law; but
let thine heart keep my
commandments . . . So shalt thou
find favour and good understanding
in the sight of God and man.

PROVERBS 3:1, 4

Take a Stand

Taking a stand for what's right can be a lonely venture in today's world. It's a job with many openings but few candidates. When we see an injustice done or something unethical proposed, the easy route is to turn a blind eye. Getting involved could be messy, after all. Yet deep inside our consciences are pricked, and we hear that still, small voice of God whispering what He requires.

The choice is ours. Will we take a stand—proving the depth of our convictions? Or will we spout idle talk about right living, without supporting those words with action?

Though taking a stand is often unpopular, it's the mark of true integrity. All who allow God to set their course know it's the only way to live. And those who scorn your values will respect you in the end.

*Let your life preach so loudly that
you never have to say a word.*

Faults are thick
where love is thin.

*Above all things have fervent
charity among yourselves:
for charity shall cover the
multitude of sins.*

1 PETER 4:8

Giving Up Revenge

The first thing we want to do when someone hurts us is to lash out. Our human nature desires revenge—or, at the very least, calculated indifference. *She deserves a taste of what she dished out,* we reason. But the kind of love God places in a heart goes against this self-protective mindset. When He moves in and dwells in our hearts, change takes place. It may take years, but change comes.

What does it mean to say that love "covers a multitude of sins"? Simply that the God type of love keeps on loving in the face of rejection, hatred, and persecution. It doesn't excuse the wrong actions of others but loves in spite of them.

Allow God's supernatural love to change you from the inside out. You may be surprised at the person you become.

Love looks over offenses and befriends anyway.

Some people reach the
top of the ladder of success
only to find it is leaning
against the wrong wall.

Seek ye first the kingdom of God,
and his righteousness; and all these
things shall be added unto you.

Success?

How do you define success? A bank vault full of money? Reaching the top rung of your career ladder? Achieving fame? Or can success be defined in simpler ways, such as seeing your children grow into Godly adults? Maybe success is enjoying what you do for a living and blessing others through it. Or maybe it can be defined as being content with what you have and knowing that you're fulfilling God's destiny for your life.

Only when we complete this earthly sojourn will we be able to fully see the big picture. Only then, when we share God's perspective on things, will we realize what true success is. He's already told us this much of the puzzle: those who give up their lives for Him will gain them in the end. Surely, that's the biggest reward of all.

Success comes when we pursue God,
not material things.

A friend is one who
comes in when the whole
world has gone out.

A friend loves at all times,
And a brother is born for adversity.

PROVERBS 17:17 NASB

Who Is Still There?

We all need friends to stand with us during our "down" times as well as our "up" ones. In fact, there's no better test of true friendship than those times when we're down and out, unable to pull ourselves up by the bootstraps. When catastrophe hits, look to see who's left standing with you. When hardship lands on your doorstep, reach out—the ones who reach back are your true friends.

This goes both ways. It's said that to have friends you must be a friend. Can others count on you when their worlds are being shattered? If you've not been as true a friend in the past as you want to be, there's always room for a new start. Reach out today to meet a friend's need—or simply listen. Sometimes, that's the best form of friendship you can offer.

A friend in need is a friend indeed.

If the grass looks greener
on the other side of the
fence, you can bet
the water bill is higher.

Let your character or moral disposition be free from love of money [including greed, avarice, lust, and craving for earthly possessions] and be satisfied with your present [circumstances and with what you have]; for He [God] Himself has said, I will not in any way fail you nor give you up nor leave you without support.

HEBREWS 13:5 AMP

116

The Gift of Contentment

A little girl peered through a toyshop window at a kitten made from a sock. Its black eyes, pink nose, and curving smile beckoned her. She begged her mother to buy it, but the mother said no. On Christmas Day, when she tore into her last present, there lay the long-sought-for kitten, grinning up at her. Her mother's eyes sparkled from across the room.

But a peculiar thing happened. The kitten lost its appeal. Now other toys beckoned her from toy shop windows. If only she could have *them!*

Years later, the girl—now a woman—came across the toy in a dresser drawer, wrapped in cloth to protect its faded yarn. She stroked the ancient face of the kitten, content now with the memory of the sparkle in her mother's eyes and this symbol of her mother's love.

Contentment with what we
have is a gift from God.

Do not in the darkness
of night what you'd
shun in broad daylight.

*The night is far spent, the day
is at hand: let us therefore cast
off the works of darkness, and let
us put on the armour of light.*

Walk in the Light

How different our behavior would be if we walked around in a spotlight or knew that our actions were being caught on video to be broadcast on the evening news! Secrecy is the ally of bad behavior. Darkness is its second cousin. But light and transparency are no threat to the one whose deeds are righteous. For that person, behavior doesn't change under the cloak of night, and they have nothing to be ashamed of or hide.

Living in the light is a figurative way of saying, "Live as if God were walking every step of the way with you." The fact is, He is. As you listen for His voice, imagine what He would do in every situation, and ask Him to help you make right decisions. When we come to God with requests like this, He is more than happy to oblige.

God is with you every step of the way today; walk in the light with courage.

Remember: the mightiest oak was once a little nut that held its ground.

Though your beginning was insignificant, Yet your end will increase greatly.

JOB 8:7 NASB

Set to God's True North

History is full of spiritual Cinderella stories—plots marked by ordinary starts, numerous pitfalls and setbacks, blinding perseverance, and stellar conclusions. Why? Because the men and women who serve as lead characters of these stories had one thing in common: a resolve to honor Him in all they did. When God is writing your book, the story is bound to turn out well.

Take courage that most of the "heroes of faith" not only had small beginnings, they had *terrible* beginnings—beginnings that might have easily discouraged the faint-hearted. Yet they also possessed a fire-in-the-bones sense of mission to answer God's call. If we could go back in time and be a fly on the wall, we'd see their doubts and insecurities. After all, they were human. But we'd also witness that each held to a steady course, with a compass set to God's true north.

Your start doesn't dictate your ending
when God is writing the plot.

We should seize every
opportunity to give
encouragement.
Encouragement is
oxygen to the soul.

*A man hath joy by the answer
of his mouth: and a word spoken
in due season, how good is it!*

PROVERBS 15:23

Oxygen to the Soul

Breathing encouragement—what a refreshing image that calls to mind. If encouragement is like good, clean oxygen to the soul, then words of discouragement are like exhaust fumes that choke our ability to breathe. You can't get too much of the first, but too much of the latter makes you sick—literally.

What's on your agenda today? Even if it's full, there's always room to squeeze in a little encouragement for the people you meet. For some this comes naturally. Words of encouragement flow from their tongues. But for others it may need to become a learned response, a catechism of kindness that prompts them to boost others whenever the opportunity arises.

Never pass up the chance to make someone's day. Doing so will boomerang blessings back to you.

Make time for encouragement,
and it will make time for you.

If you're heading in
the wrong direction,
God allows U-turns.

*If you repent, I will restore
you that you may serve me.*

JEREMIAH 15:19 NIV

Changing Course

Steering back onto the track when you've veered off is one thing; making an abrupt U-turn is quite another. Yet that's the sort of radical change encounters with God can bring about. One minute you're hurtling down a familiar but destructive path. The next moment you find yourself face to face with the Divine—and it leaves you changed for good.

When God interrupts our plans, at first we may squirm and shout like toddlers. But when He brings us into full contact with Himself, we are awed into reverence and transformed deep inside. No one who has stood in His presence remains the same. (That's why it's called Good News!)

Whatever your path today, if you're not going God's way, know that it is never too late to turn around and head in the right direction. God not only welcomes U-turns, He gently prods you toward them.

Steer the course God has set for you.
It leads to a sure destination.

Anyone can hold the helm
when the sea is calm.

*If thou faint in the day of
adversity, thy strength is small.*

PROVERBS 24:10

The Lesson of Adversity

It's easy to feel confident when everything's going your way and no waves are rocking the boat. You steer a steady course and congratulate yourself on what a fine job you're doing in life. But then adversity strikes, crashing over you like a tidal wave, and suddenly it takes all your strength just to cling to the helm and keep from capsizing. Perhaps you never saw the wave coming. Even if you did, you realized with one glance that it was big enough to drown you.

We wonder, *What kind of caring God would allow us to flounder like this?* But from the vantage point of eternity, adversity teaches us what He can do for us—and what we cannot do for ourselves. We lose our false confidence in ourselves, and we can place a well-founded confidence in Him.

When you're in the midst of a storm, remember who holds the power to calm it.

People who fly
into a rage always
make a bad landing.

One who is quick-tempered
acts foolishly.

PROVERBS 14:17 NRSV

The High Cost of Anger

Anger is a costly emotion: it bankrupts our serenity, spoils our relationships, and bumps our stress levels into high gear. Many people mistake anger for strength; they assume a loud, overbearing manner will earn them respect, but it always backfires. Sooner or later people realize that one who can't control his temper is no better than an unbroken stallion—strong and fierce but dangerous to be around.

True strength is laced with gentleness. It stands up for what's right and admits when it's wrong. A strong character may be tempted to become angry but remembers that a short fuse never solves a problem.

We all struggle to keep a lid on our anger. If your temper flares too easily, ask God to hold you accountable. Don't be afraid to practice the old remedy of counting to ten before blowing.

Tame your temper day by day; the effort it takes will yield a high return.

The discipline of desire
is the background
of character.

I keep under my body, and
bring it into subjection:
lest that by any means,
when I have preached to others,
I myself should be a castaway.

1 CORINTHIANS 9:27

The Blessing of Purity

We live in a sexually charged world that hawks sensuality from every conceivable platform. Is it any wonder that temptations abound? Even those with a strict moral code find it difficult to stay pure in thought, word, and deed. Magazine covers, television shows, movies, Web sites, and clothing trends all war against the resolve to stay on the "straight and narrow." Yet God's code of ethics remains unchanged, reminding us that cultural norms are sometimes polar opposites to the standard of purity God has set for His children.

If you choose a life of Godly living, you will stand out from the crowd—maybe even be teased for it. But every step on the path of moral behavior leads to life-long blessing. Don't be ashamed to step away from the pack. Count it a privilege to be one who upholds Godliness in a Godless culture.

Practice purity; it can become habit-forming.

The day which we
fear as our last is but
the birthday of eternity.

Teach us to number our days,
that we may apply our
hearts unto wisdom.

PSALM 90:12

Success at a Snail's Pace

Steady plodding works better than a mad dash to the finish. The first produces success and time to enjoy it; the second yields a pounding heart rate and a stressful journey. Mark your course and then stay true to it, one step at a time. Someday you'll be able to see how far you've come, traveling at this "snail's pace."

Have you ever faced a task you didn't want to do, so you wound up rushing just to be done with it? More than likely, the rush job resulted in shoddy work—work that needed redoing in the proper manner. The same applies to our lives. We can persevere, living by God's standards, or we can cut corners—but discover we've really lost time. Choose the way of that slow, plodding creature who made it to the Ark in the end!

*The road to success is paved
with perseverance.*

"Gospel" signifies good, merry, glad, and joyful tidings that make a person . . . sing, dance, and leap for joy.

Go ye into all the world, and preach the gospel to every creature.

MARK 16:15

The Good-News Cure

Why is talking about our faith so hard to do? We may easily gab about the latest technology or the best place to shop, but when the topic of God surfaces, we tend to clam up. We don't want to appear pushy, or we're afraid we'll be ridiculed for our beliefs; we worry about sounding politically incorrect or narrow-minded, or we just don't want to ruffle any feathers.

Think of your faith this way: Suppose that after much research you found a cure for cancer. You knew it saved lives, so you told everyone you met about it. Talking about the cure became your mission in life.

We forget, a life apart from God is a dire thing. But you know the key to eternal life with Him. Spread it around. Those who accept it will thank you someday in Heaven.

Good news is a delight to share—
don't keep it all to yourself!

A coincidence is a small miracle where God prefers to remain anonymous.

Who can put into words and tell the mighty deeds of the Lord? Or who can show forth all the praise [that is due Him]?

PSALM 106:2 AMP

Minimiracles

Perhaps when we're in Heaven we will realize just how many "coincidences" in this life were actually mini miracles, wrought on our behalf by attending angels. Last-minute opportunities fall into place, we make it out of close scrapes, we meet the right people at just the right time—surely there's more going on behind the scenes than meets the eye. Some call it serendipity, but it may border on the supernatural. As we meander through our workaday lives, we forget that a thin veil separates this world from the next—that God is orchestrating events even when we forget He's there.

The psalmist praised God for His mighty deeds, but we have reason to praise Him for the small acts of grace as well. As you go through this day, stop and thank God for those mini miracles occurring all around you.

The mundane becomes miraculous
when God's hand is in it.

Look up and not down;
look forward and not back;
look out and not in;
and lend a hand.

This one thing I do, forgetting
those things which are behind,
and reaching forth unto those
things which are before.

PHILIPPIANS 3:13

Leave the Past Behind

Camping out in the past is like watching grass grow: it's a big waste of time. While the past is a part of you, it's a part you can never alter, so why spend your time either anguished or overly nostalgic about it? The opportunity exists for each of us to take what is good from the past and use it to sculpt the future. By making the past a springboard, we resist the temptation to turn it into a hammock—an idle place intended only for passive contemplation.

Leave whatever you did or didn't do in the burial ground of yesterday. Instead, make a list of things you did right, times when you listened to the voice of God and followed His leading. Then move forward. Today is a new beginning. Watch for the coming blessings.

God is a present-tense Father;
meet with Him today.

Knowing and not
doing are equal to
not knowing at all.

To one who knows the right
thing to do and does not
do it, to him it is sin.

JAMES 4:17 NASB

The Right Thing to Do

Someone once said that the same opportunity never knocks twice, but there's one exception to that unwritten rule: the opportunity to do what's right. Over and over again, we face the choice to do what we know to be right and true—or not to do it. How one chooses builds a life of integrity or one that deadens the conscience and leads to regret.

Children learn this lesson early. Watch a group of toddlers playing sometime. Most won't share automatically. They have to be taught to do the right thing. If not, they pay the consequences through some type of discipline from Mom or Dad. Human nature tells them to hoard their toys and choose the best for themselves. Repeated training steers them toward the higher road until action grows into character.

Make truth and right actions a permanent part of your personality.

If you come to a fork in the road, take the "right" way.

He who is most slow
in making a promise
is the most faithful
in its performance.

*LORD, who may dwell in
your sanctuary? . . . He whose
walk is blameless . . . who keeps
his oath even when it hurts.*

PSALM 15:1-2, 4 NIV

Guard Your Word

Making promises you can't keep is serious business—especially to God. Yet the days are long gone when a person's word was his bond and deals were struck on a handshake. Why? Because little by little we have become people whose promises can't be trusted. No wonder the legal profession is such a big business! Now we are held to our oaths by a lot of fine print and financial penalties. The simple sanctity of a word of honor has vanished, a memory of days gone by.

Have you made a promise lately? Has someone asked for your discretion in a sensitive matter? Guard your word—your honor—like treasure. At the same time, use wisdom. Be slow to promise but quick to follow through when you do. You will stand out from the crowd and reflect the One who created Truth.

Honor affects your countenance
even when you're unaware of it.

The heart has no secret
which our conduct
does not reveal.

*"The good man brings good things
out of the good stored up in him,
and the evil man brings evil things
out of the evil stored up in him."*

MATTHEW 12:35 NIV

Your Heart on Your Sleeve

A storehouse holds whatever is stashed away in it. If a person fills a storehouse with auto parts, that building won't suddenly contain clothing. If a farmer fills a silo with grain, that silo won't deliver potatoes when opened. It only receives what is put into it.

The same analogy has been used for computers: input equals output. Bad information in; bad information out. Good information in; good information out. Computers are predictable in that way.

So are human beings. What we put into our hearts and minds will ultimately flow out of us, whether good or evil. Your heart can't be fooled—sooner or later it brings forth exactly what's stored inside. Want to live a good life? Spend your days cultivating Godly thoughts and committing good deeds, and that's what will come out of you.

Live righteously, and wear your heart on your sleeve.

To have one's world
centered in God is peace.

*To be carnally minded is
death; but to be spiritually
minded is life and peace.*

ROMANS 8:6

The Spring of Peace

Scripture speaks of a peace that "passeth all understanding." We long for such peace. A person may move to the country or quit a stressful job. Only, the same worries look up the forwarding address. Peace seems to be always just beyond our grasp. Or is it?

Peace is not something we can force. It springs from a heart that is centered on God. It wells up from within when we trust in His timing, His goodness, His mercy, and His promises. This supernatural kind of peace does not come from geographical changes. It comes only when we relinquish our lives to God's oversight.

Do you have worries weighing you down today? Dump them at God's feet. Don't worry—it's what He wants you to do. Repeat this action as often as needed. (Sometimes that means minute by minute!) Then peace will flow.

A peaceful heart doesn't have the word "worry" in its vocabulary.

If you want to make
an easy job seem
mighty hard, just keep
putting off doing it.

*How long are ye slack to go to
possess the land, which the LORD
God of your fathers hath given you?*

JOSHUA 18:3

Putting Things Off?

Procrastination hounds many of us, turning ordinary tasks into dreaded chores. We put off doing what we know we'll have to do eventually—and wind up even more frustrated. Then, because we waited so long, we are forced to rush the job and may even do less than our best.

Does this sound familiar?

The easiest remedy for procrastination is "stick-to-it-iveness," a determination to tackle a job head-on and see it through to the end. If sheer willpower won't work, try viewing the task as a to-do item from God Himself and "work as unto the Lord." This doesn't mean you should work as if Big Brother were watching you, motivated out of fear. Instead, the job calls up a sense of reverence in the one working. When you're toiling for God, you're performing work of the highest order.

Consider yourself an employee on God's payroll.

If the roots are deep and strong, the tree needn't worry about the wind.

Blessed is the man who trusts in the LORD . . . He will be like a tree planted by the water that sends out its roots by the stream. It does not fear when heat comes; its leaves are always green. It has no worries in a year of drought and never fails to bear fruit.

JEREMIAH 17:7-8 NIV

Deep Roots

Horticulturists tell us that letting the ground dry out thoroughly before watering deeply helps root growth and that light winds will strengthen the trunks of young saplings. By forcing them to find their own water supply, the trees' roots sink deep into the earth.

Years later, the trees will be huge, sturdy testaments to horticultural wisdom. They will be able to withstand harsh winds and water deprivation, because those little adversities will have made the trees strong enough to do so.

A life whose little problems have caused it to grow deep roots of faith in God is like a tree that stands strong, despite the storms that beat against it. It may bend and sway when pounded by the elements, but it only grows deeper roots and a sturdier trunk as a result.

Little troubles send your faith deep—so you grow able to survive the big ones.

I never made a sacrifice. We ought not to talk of sacrifice when we remember the great sacrifice that he made who left his Father's throne on high to give himself for us.

To win the contest you must deny yourselves many things that would keep you from doing your best.

1 CORINTHIANS 9:25 TLB

God's Got Your Number

Being your best is easier said than done when the frozen waffles burn, the kids are screaming, and traffic comes to a standstill. We all get frustrated with life's daily struggles. Sometimes we blow those struggles out of proportion, and they threaten to ruin the day, the week—even the whole year. Bumping along in low gear, we wonder: *where's the peace that passes all understanding when we need it?*

Don't ever forget that God's got your number. Though life can throw curveballs, you're in the best position to catch them on the fly when you start each day by relinquishing your life to Him. God promises to be strong in your weakness if you give Him your whole self. How do we tap into His strength? Surrender and trust. Wait for His answer like you mean it.

When the pressure hits, surrender immediately—to Him.

Things human must be
known to be loved;
things Divine must be
loved to be known.

The fool hath said in his heart,
There is no God.

PSALM 14:1

Handwriting on the Wall

God leaves His fingerprints all around us. Though He is sometimes silent in our lives, traces of His presence are everywhere. You walk outside on a starry night and see His handiwork in the sky. A friend calls at just the right moment to pray for you, and it seems to be more than coincidence. You circle the parking lot on your way to the foot doctor and find a space right in front of the door. A child smiles at you in the park.

No matter where you go or what you do today, remember that Someone is watching out for you and sending you "postcards" of His presence. Be on the lookout for them. God scribbles love notes on the world around us, but it's up to us to read them—and claim them as our own.

Serenity is when we see the handwriting on the wall and know it's meant for us.

Whatever comes,
let's be content withall:
Among God's blessings
there is no one small.

Because the Lord is my Shepherd,
I have everything I need!

PSALM 23:1 TLB

All You Need

Contentment is one of those elusive traits we esteem in others but find difficult to cultivate in our own lives. We may fool ourselves into believing that we are content, but we catch ourselves pining away for yet another "toy." Words written more than two thousand years ago still echo down through the ages with simple, Godly wisdom: *Because I am God's, I have everything I need.*

Are those words true for you today? Do you have everything you need? Often, we define *need* as *want.* But God promises to feed, clothe, and shelter His children—to take care of their *needs.* When we put Him first, He also promises to pour blessings beyond our needs.

Any self-respecting shepherd makes sure his lambs are cared for. Trust your life—every worrisome detail—to the Shepherd who made you for green pastures.

God will supply your every need.

Acknowledgments

Joseph Addison (12), Ben Franklin (18), Amos Traver (20), Henry Ward Beecher (24,54), John Baillie (28), Albert Schweitzer (38), Hannah More (42), Josh Billings (44), Martin Luther (46), Francis de Sales (48), Lewis Cass (50), Ralph Waldo Emerson (58,94), Saint Augustine (60), Horatio Bonar (70), Dwight L. Moody (72), George Chapman (80), Ignacy Paderewski, adapted (84), Thomas Jefferson (88), William James (90), Mae West (92), Syrus (100), William Shakespeare (104,108), Thomas Carlyle (106), James Howell (110), Alban Goodier (114), Charles Spurgeon (118), George M. Adams (122), Publilius Syrus (126), Will Rogers (128), John Locke (130), Seneca (132), William Tyndale (134), Theodore Roosevelt (138), Jean Jacques Rousseau (142), Donald Hankey (146), David Livingstone (152), Blaise Pascal (154), Robert Herrick (156).

References

Unless otherwise indicated, all Scripture quotations are taken from the *King James Version* of the Bible.

Scripture quotations marked AMP are taken from *The Amplified Bible. Old Testament* copyright © 1965, 1987 by Zondervan Corporation, Grand Rapids, Michigan. *New Testament* copyright © 1958, 1987 by the Lockman Foundation, La Habra, California. Used by permission.

Verses marked TLB are taken from *The Living Bible,* © 1971. Used by permission of Tyndale House Publishers, Inc., Wheaton, Illinois 60189. All rights reserved.

Scripture quotations marked NASB are taken from the *New American Standard Bible.* Copyright © The Lockman Foundation 1960, 1962, 1963, 1968, 1971, 1972, 1973, 1975, 1977, 1995. Used by permission.

Scripture quotation marked NKJV are taken from *The New King James Version.* Copyright © 1979, 1980, 1982, 1994, Thomas Nelson, Inc.

Scripture quotations marked NIV are taken from the *Holy Bible, New International Version®.* NIV®. Copyright © 1973, 1978, 1984 by International Bible Society. Used by permission of Zondervan Publishing House. All rights reserved.

Scripture quotations marked NRSV are from the *New Revised Standard Version* of the Bible, copyright © 1989 by The Division of Christian Education of the National Council of the Churches of Christ in the USA. Used by permission. All rights reserved.

Scriptures marked NCV are quoted from *The Holy Bible, New Century Version,* copyright © 1987, 1988, 1991 by Word Publishing, Dallas, Texas 75039. Used by permission.

Additional copies of this book
are available from your local bookstore.

Also available:

The Pocket Devotional
The Pocket Devotional for Mothers
The Pocket Devotional for Teens

as well as

My Personal Promise Bible for Women
Quiet Moments with God for Women
Everyday Prayers for Everyday Cares for Women
God's Little Devotional Book for Women
God's Little Devotional Book for Women—
Special Gift Edition
God's Little Devotional Journal for Women
God's Little Lessons for Women

If you have enjoyed this book, or if it has impacted
your life, we would like to hear from you.

Please contact us at:

Honor Books
4050 Lee Vance View
Colorado Springs, CO 80918